Putting Up With Others

Written and Illustrated by
Ron and Rebekah Coriell

Fleming H. Revell Company
Old Tappan, New Jersey

© 1981 Fleming H. Revell Company
All rights reserved
Printed in the United States of America

Forgive
give

Treating Someone as Though He Never Hurt Me

> Forbearing one another, and forgiving one another, if any man have a quarrel against any: even as Christ forgave you, so also do ye.
>
> Colossians 3:13

Forgiveness in the Bible

Fear gripped the heart of Jacob as he looked into the distant hills. Coming toward him was his brother, Esau, and 400 warriors. It had been many years since Jacob had deceived his brother and had stolen the inheritance from him.

Now Jacob was fearful that Esau was coming to kill him. He immediately began to make plans to gain his brother's forgiveness. He sent herds of sheep as presents for Esau. He also arranged his family into a long column. The first in line were the handmaids and their children. His wife Leah and her children were next. Then came Rachel and her son, Joseph. Perhaps Jacob thought that Esau would take pity on him if he saw the many children God had given him.

As Esau approached, Jacob humbly bowed before him seven times. Then Esau ran to meet him and hugged and kissed him. Both wept.

Esau asked about all the people he saw. Jacob explained how God had richly blessed him. He offered his brother the gift of the herds of sheep. Esau replied that he had enough sheep of his own. Nevertheless, Jacob urged him to accept them, and he did.

Jacob had expected his brother to come to him in anger and bitterness. To his surprise, Esau came with a forgiving spirit. He even offered to send his warriors with Jacob, to protect his family and animals on their journey. Esau had truly forgiven Jacob. He treated Jacob as if Jacob had never hurt him.

Forgiveness
of a Hero of the Faith

The crowd of Puritans cheered as the whip slashed into Obadiah's bare back. These people were glad to see him being punished for not believing as they did.

Years before, Obadiah Holmes, our country's first glassmaker, had come to New England to escape religious persecution. As a Baptist, his beliefs were not approved by the government of England; nor were they approved by the Puritans, who governed the colony where Obadiah had settled. Therefore he moved away to Newport, Rhode Island, where he could worship as he wished.

As each slash of the whip became more painful, Obadiah thought back to the events that had caused his return to Puritan country. He and two other Baptists had come to visit an old friend. While in his home, they prayed and fellowshipped together. Then they were arrested for holding a Baptist service. All three were placed in jail for ten days. Later Obadiah's two companions were released, but he was required to pay a fine or be publicly whipped. Mr. Holmes refused to pay, because he had committed no crime. Therefore he spent thirty more days in jail. He prepared himself with many hours of prayer. Then he was taken to the whipping post and flogged.

After receiving thirty strokes, he was freed. Yet, in spite of the pain and the injustice done to him, he was not bitter. Obadiah Holmes, an ancestor of Abraham Lincoln, turned to his persecutors and responded with a forgiving spirit, "You have struck me with roses."

Forgiveness at Home

Fran marched into the living room and flung herself onto the couch. The scowl on her face showed that she was upset.

"What is bothering you?" asked Father.

"I am still mad," answered Fran. "My best friend, Ronda, took Judy to the zoo after she had promised that she would take me. I've tried to take your advice, Father, and forgive her, but I just cannot seem to do it. Now she wants me to come to her birthday party, and I'm still feeling hurt."

"I understand your dilemma," comforted Father. "I have also found it hard to forgive at times. Someone once gave me a tip that has helped me. Would you like to hear it?"

Father continued, "The Bible says that it is easy to love someone who does good to you. However, in Luke 6:27 it states, 'Love your enemies, do good to them.' This means that God expects us to do good things for those who have wronged us. I found that it was easier to forgive people who hurt me if I did good things for them."

Fran was really surprised by her father's suggestion.

"What kind of good things can I do for Ronda?" she asked.

"To begin," said Father, "you can accept her party invitation. Then take her an extraspecial gift. Speak to her with kind words and a smile and treat her as if she has never hurt you. Also pray for the Lord to bless her with good things."

Fran took her father's wise counsel. During the birthday party, she felt a flood of forgiveness fill her heart.

Forgiveness at School

"He that covereth a transgression seeketh love; but he that repeateth a matter separateth very friends" (Proverbs 17:9).

Fran was taught the meaning of this Bible verse very clearly at school during recess.

"Fran!" shouted her friend Ronda. "Did you hear what Brenda did to me? She lied and told my teacher that I was throwing paper in class. Actually I wasn't."

Disappointed that she had heard this evil report about Brenda, Fran asked, "Have you forgiven her?"

"Oh, yes, of course," her friend replied.

"Have you told your other friends what Brenda did to you?" Fran asked.

"Well, yes," replied Ronda. "I wanted them to know that Brenda was a liar."

Fran then realized why all her friends seemed to be acting so rude toward Brenda lately. They refused to play with her and spoke very little to her.

"Ronda," said Fran, "I don't think you have forgiven Brenda."

"What do you mean?" asked Ronda with a surprised look.

"If you had forgiven Brenda, you would not give an evil report about her to your friends. True forgiveness is when you treat someone as though she never hurt you," said Fran.

After school, Ronda thanked Fran for her wise words. She had already apologized to her friends for the evil report that she had given. Before she left she said to Fran, "Thank you for teaching me what it means to truly forgive."

Fair
care

Treating Others Equally

. . . that thou observe these things without preferring one before another, doing nothing by partiality.

1 Timothy 5:21

Fairness in the Bible

The ruins of Ziklag were still smoldering as David and his men returned home. Not only was the entire city destroyed, but all the women and children had been taken away by the wicked Amalekites.

David gathered his 600 warriors and hurried to find the Amalekites. It was a long, hard march. David urged them to walk so fast that 200 of them became exhausted. He allowed them to stay behind and guard the baggage. With the rest of the warriors, David continued. They found a sick boy who was a slave to an Amalekite. He had been left behind to die. David helped the lad to recover, and in return the boy led them to the Amalekite camp.

David's army bravely attacked. It took an entire day of fierce fighting to destroy the enemy. When the battle ended, David was able to release all the captive women and children, unharmed.

Great joy filled the soldiers' hearts as they returned home to Ziklag. They brought with them much booty, consisting of flocks and herds of cattle. However, when they rejoined the 200 men who had been exhausted and left behind, some did not want to share the booty with them.

David had a sense of fairness. He knew that these men had armed themselves willingly and had marched with him after the Amalekites. Therefore he rewarded these men equally.

Fairness
of a Hero of the Faith

As the missionary George Grenfell talked with the friendly African chief, sounds of sobbing pierced the air. Making his way through the crowd, Mr. Grenfell found two little girls bound with cords and tied to a tree. He learned that they had been stolen from a rival tribe and were tied up to be sold as slaves.

George Grenfell realized how unfair it was to enslave people. Therefore he offered the chief some cloth and beads and bought the two young captives. In his heart, he hoped to be able to find their native village and set them free.

Later, as Mr. Grenfell traveled down river in his steamer, the *S. S. Peace*, they were attacked by natives in a whole fleet of canoes. They threw spears and shot poison-tipped arrows. Many stuck in the sides of the *Peace*, and one almost struck George Grenfell. Suddenly one of the little slave girls began to shout and wave excitedly.

"That is my brother, and this is my home!" she cried.

"Then call to him and attract his attention!" said Mr. Grenfell.

The girl shouted as loudly as she could, but the noise of the attacking warriors drowned out her words. Only when a blast from the steamer's whistle was given did the natives fall silent long enough to hear the little girl. Immediately they put down their weapons and welcomed the missionary and his crew to their village.

Because George Grenfell was fair in his treatment of the captive girls, he was able to win the confidence of these warlike Africans and begin to witness for Christ in their village.

Fairness at Home

Larry Morgan raced through the house, making sure that everything looked just right. The tables were set, the hot dogs were ready, and the decorations were just right. He was sure that his birthday party was going to be a success.

The doorbell rang, and Larry ran to open it. The friends he had invited had started to arrive.

"Welcome," he said proudly. "I'm so glad you could come."

As his friends came, during the next fifteen minutes, Larry's excitement grew. Each brought him a birthday present. Larry made it a point to be extra friendly to some of his friends who were from wealthy families. They brought large gifts, and he wanted to be sure that they had a good time. On the other hand, he paid little attention to a church friend who was from a poor family. His clothes were faded, and he only brought Larry a birthday card. When seats were assigned at lunch, his church friend was placed at the far end of the table, while Larry sat at the other end, close to his wealthy friends.

Larry's parents watched his behavior throughout the party. They became aware of the unfairness with which he was treating his friend from church. At a convenient time, they drew Larry aside and rebuked him for not treating his friends equally. Larry was ashamed of his behavior. After asking God's forgiveness, he rejoined the party. This time he paid equal attention to everyone.

Fairness at School

Larry watched the soccer ball swish into the back of the net.
"Goal!" shouted a teammate.
"Great shot!" called another.
Graham Hill had just scored his sixth goal of the game. His gym-class team had won the game 6-0.

Larry's teammates all tried to sit next to Graham, in the locker room, afterwards. They crowded around and asked him all kinds of questions. Graham was a celebrity not only because of his soccer skills, but also because he was from England.

In school Graham received the same special treatment. Larry's best friends no longer cared to walk with him in the halls. They did not even show any interest in eating lunch with him. Everyone wanted to be around Graham.

Larry noticed that some of this attention to the English boy caused strife. Two boys got into a fight over who would play alongside of Graham in the next gym class. Boys who always were close friends no longer treated each other with kindness. Even the girls seemed to show an unusual interest in Graham.

As he thought about it, Larry felt that it was unfair for friends to be neglecting each other and even fighting, just to gain the interest of the new boy. He remembered what the Scripture said in James 3:17: "The wisdom that is from above is . . . without partiality. . . ."

Larry then purposed in his heart not to give special attention to just one person, but rather to be fair to all his friends and treat them equally.

Tolerant
elephant

Accepting Others, Even if They Are Different

My brethren, have not the faith of our Lord Jesus Christ, the Lord of glory, with respect of persons.

James 2:1

Tolerance in the Bible

"Verily I say unto you, that one of you shall betray me" (Matthew 26:21).

Shock and sorrow filled the disciples around the Passover table. They began to ask one another whom it could be. Judas Iscariot knew that Jesus was referring to him.

Three years before, he had been chosen to be a disciple. *Disciple* means "learner." Throughout those years, Judas had learned much about Jesus; nevertheless, he never accepted Christ as his personal Lord and Saviour. Jesus was well aware of this, yet He still tolerated Judas in His company.

Judas' name is the Greek form of the Hebrew name *Judah*, a very honorable Jewish name. But Judas was a dishonorable man. He was the treasurer of the money that was collected by the other disciples. Jesus knew that Judas was a thief and had taken some of the funds for himself. In spite of this, Jesus treated Judas in the same way He did the rest of the disciples.

As the Passover supper progressed, Jesus took some bread and dipped it into the meat sauce and gave it to Judas. This was a gesture that a person makes to a special friend. Jesus was aware that Judas had met with the wicked religious leaders in Jerusalem and that Judas had agreed to betray Him. Nevertheless, He did not reveal this to the rest of His friends at the table. He just told Judas to go do quickly what he was going to do.

Jesus tolerated Judas with full knowledge that his actions would lead to His crucifixion and death.

Tolerance
of a Hero of the Faith

The brave missionary couple had endured storms, been nearly shipwrecked, and had eaten endless meals of cornmeal mush with molasses. After four months at sea, John Clough and his wife arrived in India.

The mission station at Ongole was known as the Forlorn Hope, because over the years few had been won to Christ. On three occasions the mission agency considered abandoning the work. As the Cloughs began their ministry in 1864 they knew that they would need God's grace and power. Because of the caste system in India at that time, the different social classes of people did not associate. Soon some rich people of India informed the Cloughs that they would not become Christians if they had to associate with Christians who were poor people.

John Clough asked himself, *Must I forbid poor people to become church members in order to receive into membership one rich Indian?* It was an old and difficult problem in India.

Then one day he and his wife read 1 Corinthians 1:27, 28. "But God hath chosen the . . . base things of the world, and things which are despised. . . ." The Cloughs made the crucial decision to tolerate all the people, rich or poor, and seek to win them to Christ and allow them to join the mission church.

From that moment on, God blessed the work in a mighty way. All Indians were accepted as worthy to hear the Gospel and worthy for consideration for church membership. By 1882, there were 20,865 Christians associated with the mission station that was once called the Forlorn Hope.

Tolerance at Home

At last Raymond had arrived at church camp. This was the day for which he had been waiting.

As his parents unpacked the car, Raymond hustled to the camp office to get his cabin assignment. He wondered whom he would get for a bunkmate. Great disappointment swept over him as he read whom it would be.

"Oh, no," he moaned. "How could they do this to me? They have assigned me to bunk with Chester Staley."

When Raymond returned to the car, Father asked him why he looked so sad.

Raymond replied, "I'm not going to stay. Let's just pack up and go home."

"Wait just a minute," protested his father. "Your camp fee was paid months ago. You can't back out now. What is the matter?"

Raymond then explained that Chester was the messiest camper every year. He always kept his cabin from getting enough points to win in the cleanest-cabin contest.

"Well, all I can say, Son, is what the Bible says," counseled Father. "It says that we are to 'forbear one another.' This means that we are to be tolerant of others who are different from us. Perhaps you can make it your goal to help Chester be a little neater."

Raymond was finally convinced to give camp a try.

Raymond's tolerance encouraged Chester to be more orderly. As a result, their cabin was runner-up for the cleanest-cabin award.

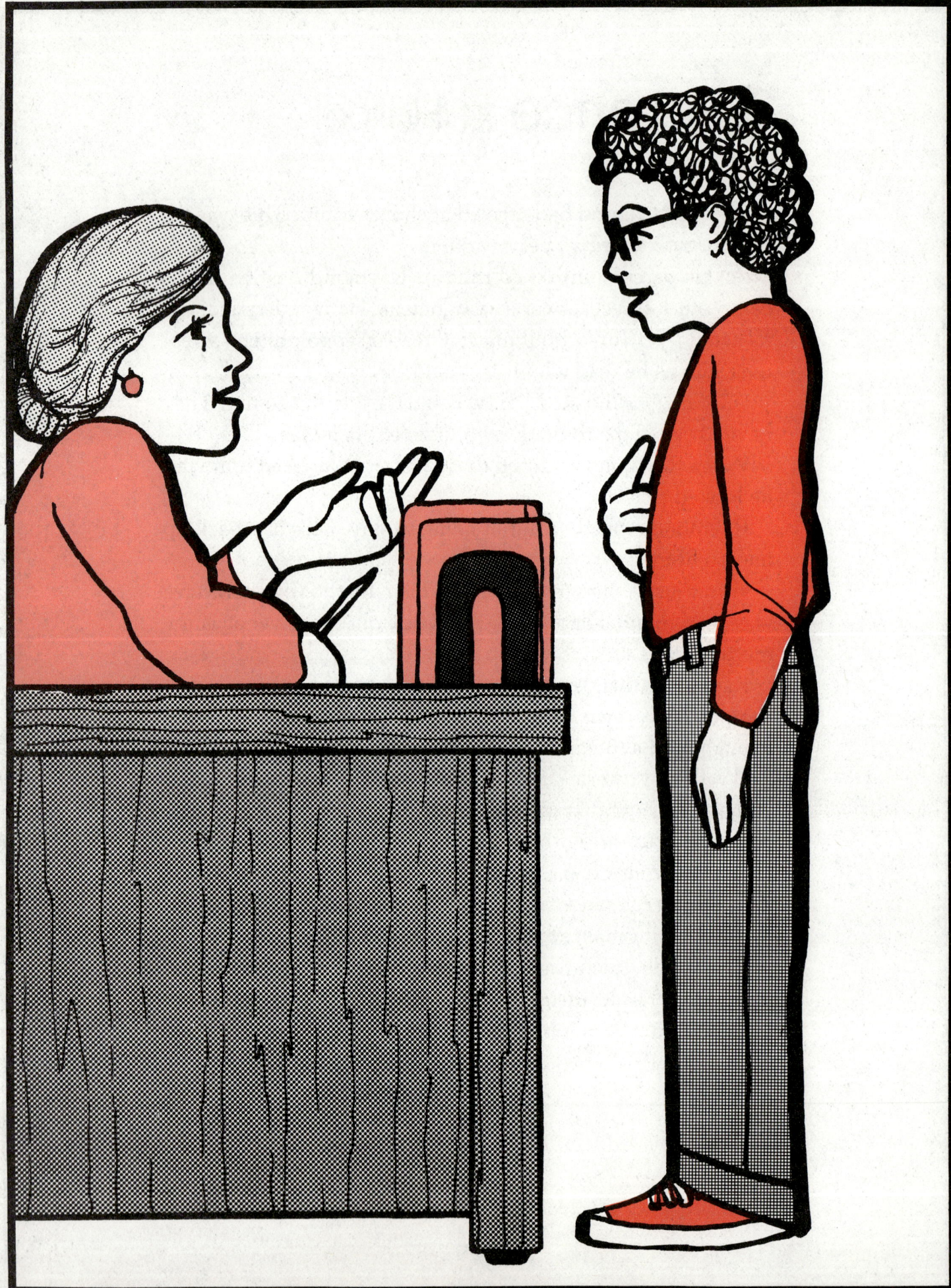

Tolerance at School

"Raymond, I would like to see you after school today," said his teacher, Mrs. Thorn.

Raymond swallowed hard and quietly said, "Yes, ma'am." He wondered what he had done to deserve this. He could not recall breaking any of the rules.

After school he waited for the other students to leave, and then he went up to Mrs. Thorn's desk.

"Raymond," she began, "you are a class leader. Everyone likes you and respects you. I want to give you a special assignment."

Raymond listened with a sense of relief.

"I'm sure you realize that Hector is not liked by very many of your classmates," she said. "In fact I don't know if he has any friends at all. Perhaps it is because he tries to show off, and brags a lot. I think he needs someone to encourage him to do right. But, at first, that person will have to be tolerant of some of his ways."

It was indeed a hard assignment for Raymond. He too disliked Hector, and most of the time he did not accept him. However, because Mrs. Thorn asked and because he knew it was the right thing to do, Raymond accepted the challenge.

During the next few weeks, Raymond had many opportunities to show tolerance toward Hector. Hector's behavior did not change, but Raymond's attitude toward him did.

Raymond learned that tolerating someone does not necessarily change that person. Yet Raymond changed his attitude to one of love, because he was able to accept someone, even though he was different.

Character Development Challenges

This page is designed to give parents and teachers practical suggestions for teaching character traits to children.

Forgiveness

1. The student should discover three reasons the Bible says to forgive others:
   a. Matthew 6:14
   b. Luke 6:35-37
   c. 2 Corinthians 2:10, 11
2. Jesus said we are to forgive our brother seventy times seven. To make the student aware of how often we are to forgive, have him write out the word *forgive* four hundred and ninety times.
3. The student should memorize Matthew 18:23-35. Recite the verses before the class or the church.

Fairness

1. The student should think of a situation at home or at school that is unfair. He should find a solution and apply it.
2. The student should write a one-act play or skit in which the moral is fairness. Perform it before the classroom or family.
3. The student should draw a picture in which fairness is demonstrated.

Tolerance

1. Find an older person who needs companionship. Ask the student to give one-half hour of his time to read and converse with the senior citizen.
2. Invite missionaries into the classroom or home. Encourage the missionary to share from his experience how God gave him the love and tolerance to minister to people in a different country and culture.
3. Pray daily with the student for a person whom he needs to tolerate. He should thank God for that person and ask God to bless that person's life.

Faithful Followers

Written and Illustrated by
Ron and Rebekah Coriell

Fleming H. Revell Company
Old Tappan, New Jersey

© 1980 Fleming H. Revell Company
All rights reserved.
Printed in the United States of America

Meek
leak

Patience Without Anger

To speak evil of no man, to be no brawlers, but gentle, showing all meekness unto all men.

Titus 3:2

Meekness in the Bible

Sarah stood fearfully at the door of the tent. The officers of Pharaoh had come to take her with them. Abraham comforted her as best he could and then motioned her to go. Sarah, Abraham's wife, was being taken to the Egyptian king to become one of his many wives.

It all began when a famine arose in the land of Canaan. Abraham brought his wife and belongings to Egypt, where there was food. He realized how beautiful Sarah was and became fearful that the Egyptians would kill him because they would want his wife. Abraham told Sarah to say that she was his sister. The officers of Pharaoh quickly spotted her and recommended her to the king. The ruler sent word to Abraham that he wanted Sarah to become part of his harem. In return, he would give Abraham sheep, oxen, donkeys, camels and slaves. Abraham agreed to this.

Sarah could have spoken out in anger at the dishonesty of her husband. Abraham was sinning against God and his wife. Nevertheless, Sarah's spirit was one of meekness. She resolved to be patient without anger and to trust God to work things out for good.

In time, God revealed the deception to Pharaoh. Angrily, Pharaoh returned Sarah to Abraham and scolded him for his trickery. He then commanded them to leave the land.

Just as He protected Sarah, God will take care of those who have the strength to be meek.

This story is found in Genesis 12:10-20.

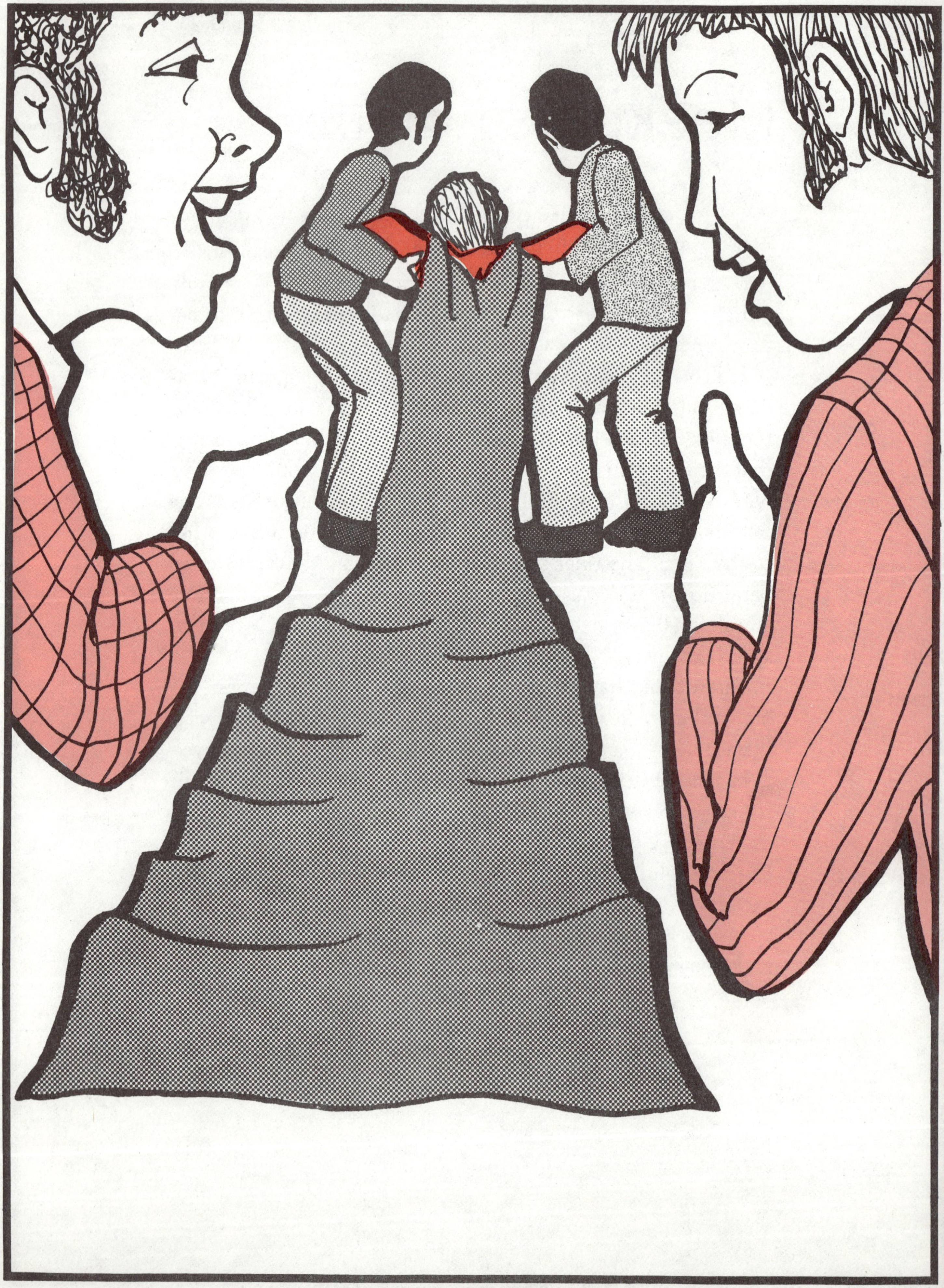

Meekness
of a Hero of the Faith

Young Jonathan Goforth looked forward to college. There he hoped to be trained for missionary work and to meet and fellowship with other Christians. To his surprise, he received an unfriendly reception.

Walking onto campus in his homemade clothes, he quickly became the object of ridicule. Even though he was poor, Jonathan determined to correct the situation. He purchased a quantity of cloth to take to a city seamstress who would make him a new wardrobe.

Learning about his plans, his classmates took him from his room by force and put his head through a hole they had cut in one end of the material. Then they made him drag the cloth up and down the hall as they mocked him. Jonathan was humiliated. He could not believe this could happen at a Christian college.

Most people would have responded by becoming either very angry or discouraged. However, Goforth was no common man. Jonathan had the inner strength to be meek. He spent hours studying his Bible and praying for his classmates.

His training in meekness prepared him to be mightily used of God in China during the early nineteenth century.

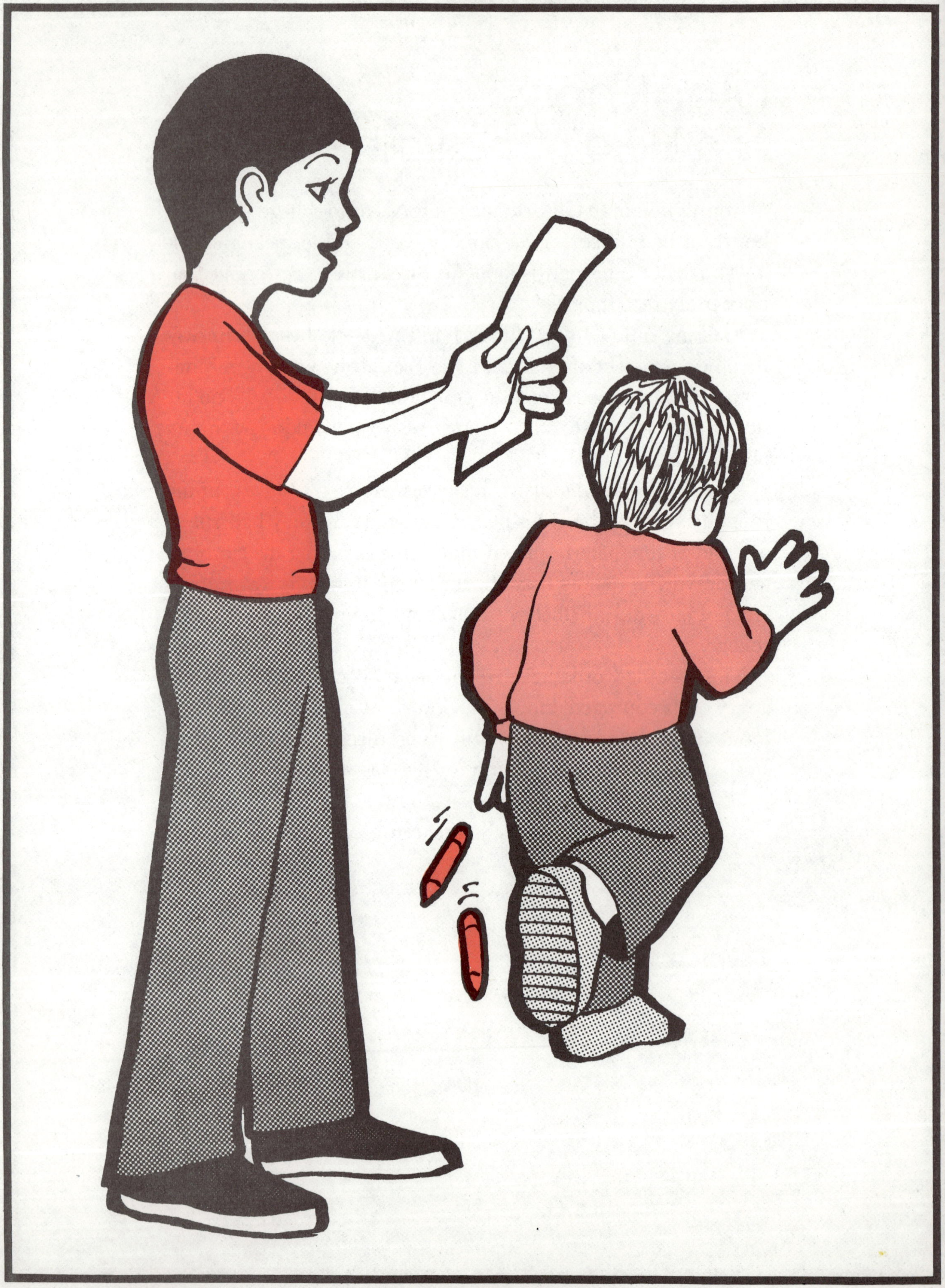

Meekness at Home

Tracey was so proud of the composition he had written in school. His teacher had allowed him to read it to the class. When school was over, he couldn't wait to get home to show it to his mother and father.

However, when he arrived home, Tracey became involved in helping his father wash and wax the new family car. He forgot about his composition until suppertime.

As Mother told them it was time to eat Tracey remembered his paper and ran up to his bedroom to get it. He was shocked when he found it.

"Oh, no!" he exclaimed. "It has crayon marks all over it!"

Angry thoughts raced through Tracey's mind. His younger brother, Joey, ran from the room. Tracey just stood there looking at his paper.

"Dear Lord," prayed Tracey. "You know how hard I worked on this composition. You also know how much I wanted Mother and Father to see and hear it. Now Joey has colored on it. I know it is wrong to stay angry with Joey. Please help me to be meek about this. Amen."

Praying when he felt angry helped Tracey to control his feelings. He decided it was still a good composition, even with Joey's artwork. So he went downstairs to eat and read his paper to the family.

There are times when it is easy to get angry. That is just the time to pray and ask God to help you to be meek.

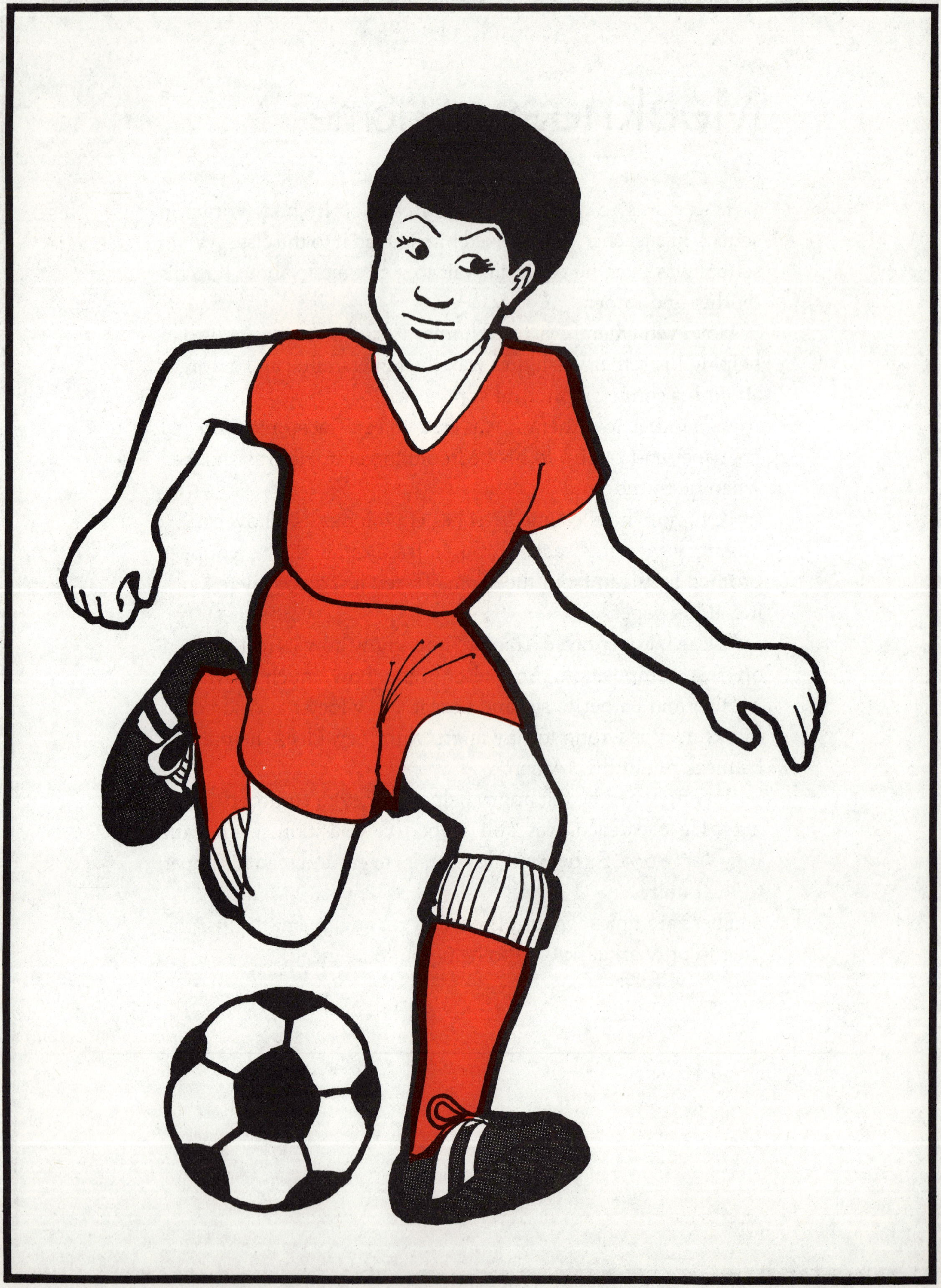

Meekness at School

Time was running out. Tracey's school soccer team was behind by only one goal.

If someone would just kick the ball my way, he thought as he ran toward the other team's goal.

Suddenly the soccer ball came toward Tracey. He stopped it with his foot and whirled around. An opponent rushed up to take it away, but Tracey expertly pushed the ball to the side and dribbled around him. He sensed that there must be only a few seconds on the clock. He swung his right foot into the ball as hard as he could, hoping his shot would get past the goalie. The ball was heading for the corner of the net when it curved slightly and bounced off the goalpost, out of bounds. Time ran out.

A great feeling of disappointment swept over Tracey. His shot had almost tied the score. Now the game was over. There was nothing more to do but shake hands.

As the boys intermingled, the winners began to laugh and jeer at Tracey's team.

"Lord, help me to be meek," he prayed. "They are acting as if they won a huge victory."

When the congratulations were finished, the winning coach came over to the bench were Tracey was sitting. "Young man," he said, "it takes someone very strong to be meek in defeat. I respect the way you acted when my boys gave you trouble."

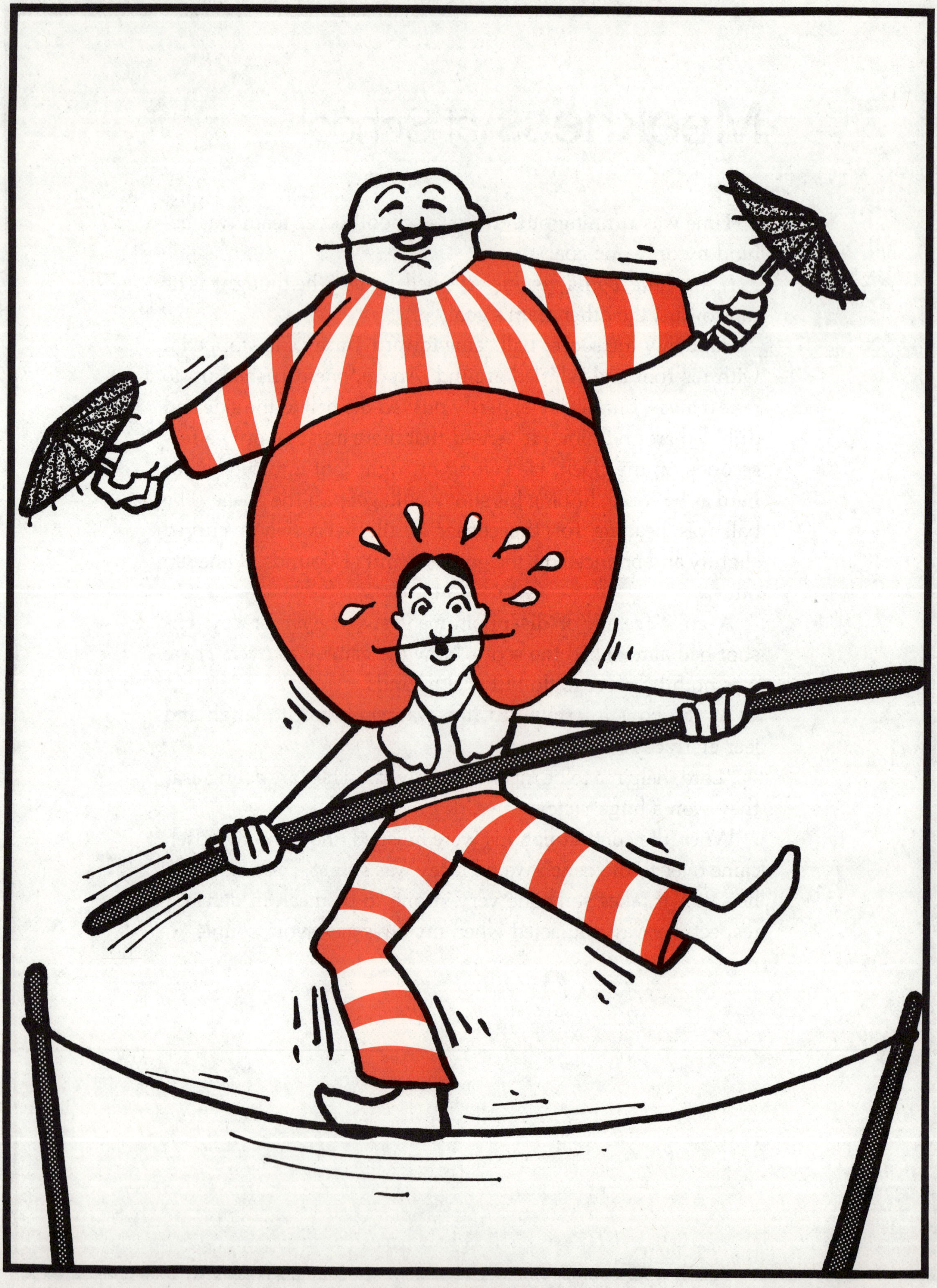

Loyal
toil

Supporting Someone
Even When the Going Gets Tough

For we are made partakers of
Christ, if we hold the beginning
of our confidence stedfast unto
the end.
                    Hebrews 3:14

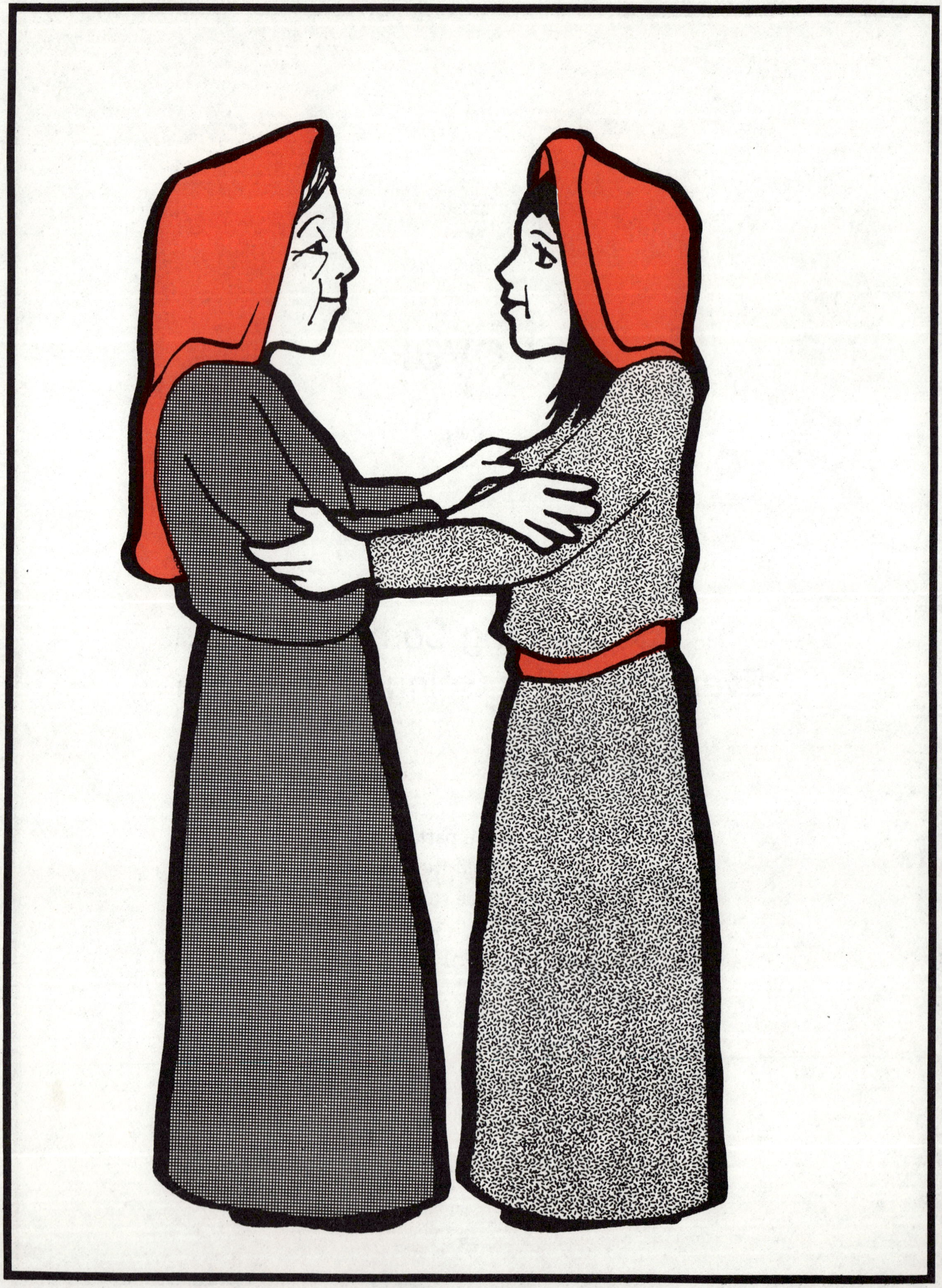

Loyalty in the Bible

Long ago, when the judges ruled in Israel, a Hebrew and his family left Bethlehem. This man had a wife named Naomi, and two sons. They traveled to Moab to escape the famine in Israel. While they were living there, the husband died. Later, Naomi's sons married two women of Moab. But soon the sons died. Grief-stricken, Naomi decided to return to her homeland without her daughters-in-law.

"My daughters," she announced, "I must return to Bethlehem. But your home is here in Moab. Stay here."

Naomi kissed them and all three women began to cry.

"Mother," the daughters-in-law cried, "we will return with you. We love you."

Naomi shook her head. "No, you must not. Perhaps you will find new husbands here, if you stay."

One daughter-in-law, Orpah, was persuaded to stay and kissed Naomi and left. But Ruth embraced Naomi and begged to go with her to Bethlehem.

"I will go wherever you go, I will live where you live, your people will become my people, and your God will be my God," said Ruth (Ruth 1:16).

When Naomi observed Ruth's loyalty, she no longer tried to persuade her to leave. Together they returned to Bethlehem.

Ruth's loyal support of her mother-in-law when she had no hope of ever being married again was rewarded. God gave her a husband and children who were to become the ancestors of Jesus Christ.

This story is found in Ruth 1:1-22.

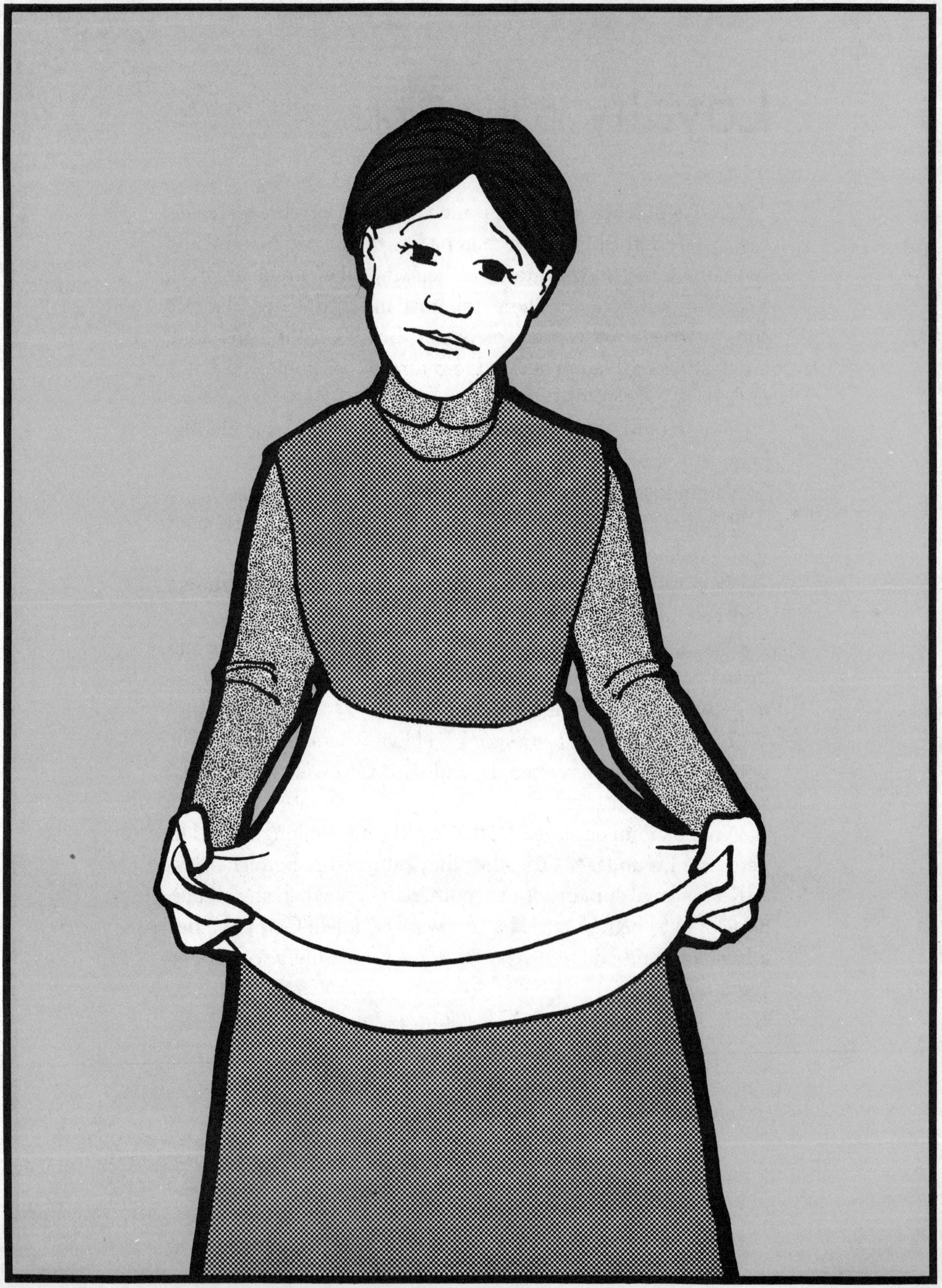

Loyalty of a Hero of the Faith

Elizabeth Bunyan was faced with a difficult decision. She could free her husband from jail, if she would convince him to change his godly convictions.

The government decreed that all clergy had to be licensed to preach. Reverend John Bunyan believed that the right to preach came only from God, not the government. Therefore, he refused to obtain a license, and, as a result, he was put in the Bedford jail.

The judge gave instructions to place a license within John's reach, just outside his cell. As soon as he signed the paper, he would be set free.

Six months passed, and the preacher would not sign. Officials came to Elizabeth Bunyan, hoping to persuade her to get her husband to sign. "No one can affect John as you can, Mrs. Bunyan," they said. "Urge him to sign. It won't hurt him."

Without her husband to support her, much of the time Mrs. Bunyan and her family were destitute. They had to rely on the help of church friends for food and clothes.

She told the men, "I have a very sick daughter, who is dying. My heart is grieved that my husband will not be able to hold her in his arms as she passes out into eternity."

But Mrs. Bunyan was a hearty woman.

Holding out the little apron she wore, she continued, "I would rather see John's head severed from his neck and in my apron than see him sign that license."

Mrs. Bunyan remained loyal to her husband's wish.

It was thirteen years before her husband was released. He never signed the license. Through those difficult times, Elizabeth Bunyan's loyalty to her husband never wavered.

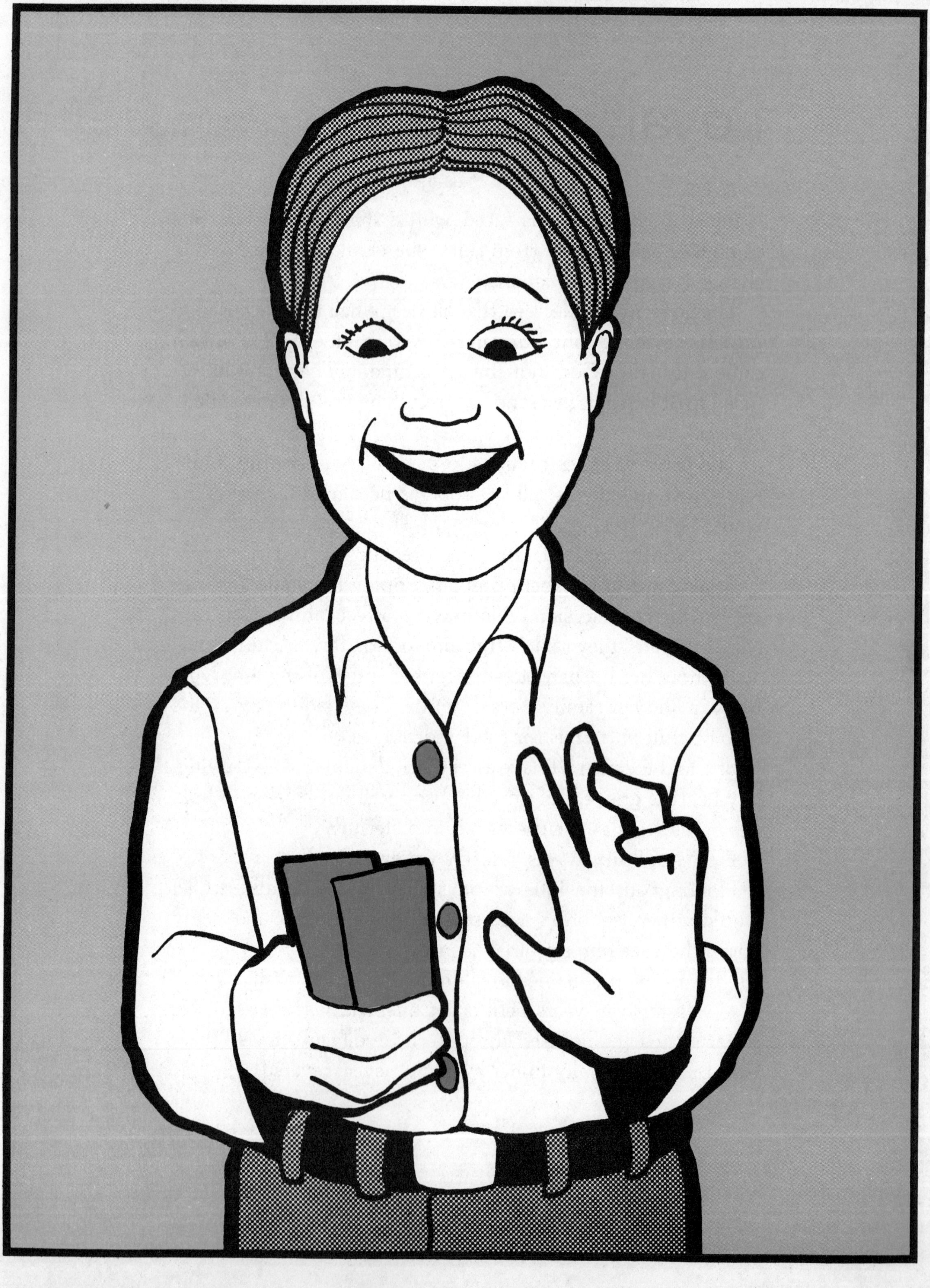

Loyalty at Home

"Wow!" shouted Jack. "Tickets to a pro basketball game. This is something I've wanted to do all year. Who gave them to us, Father?"

"They are from your Uncle Fred," replied Father. "He sometimes gets free tickets at the place where he works."

"Can we go?" asked Jack with excitement. "We can never afford to buy our own tickets. This will probably be the only time this year we will get to go. Please, can we go?"

"Calm down, Son. I think you have forgotten what day this is. This is Sunday. You know we always go to church. We would have to miss the morning service in order to drive into town to get to the game."

"I know, Father," replied Jack. "But couldn't we skip just this once?"

"Let me ask you, Son," said Father; "would we be loyal to the Lord and to our church if we did not attend because of a basketball game? To be loyal means to support someone even when the going gets tough. I know it is difficult to pass up using these tickets, but our church needs our attendance each Sunday. In that way, we are supporting it."

Jack was disappointed, but he knew that his father was right. The Lord would be sad if Jack chose to go to a basketball game instead of hearing His Word. Jack decided it was better to be loyal to the Lord than to be entertained at a basketball game.

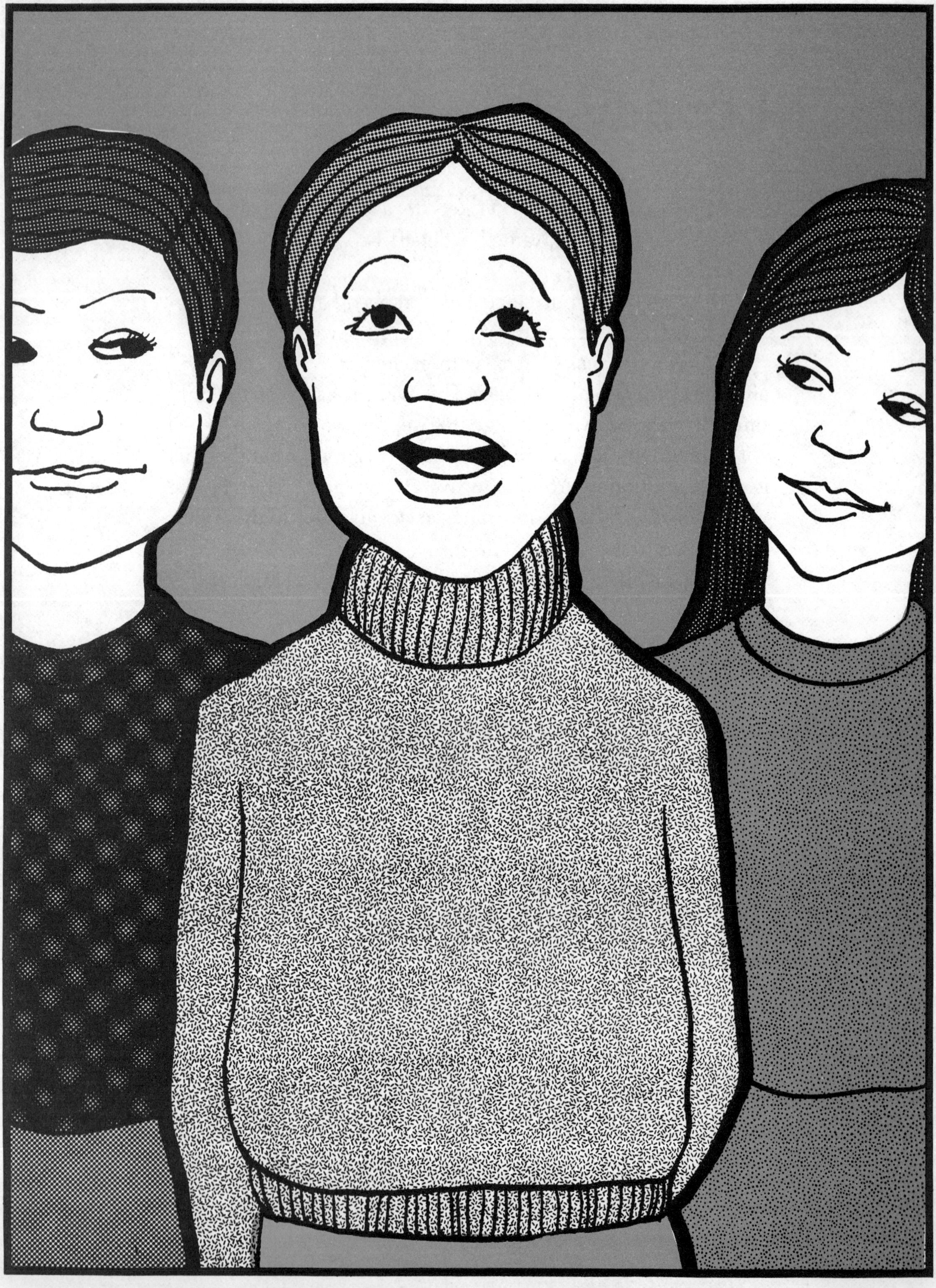

Loyalty at School

The excitement before the school basketball game was a thrill for Jack. The pep band played loudly and cheerleaders led the crowd in thunderous cheers. When the players' warm-up drills were over, an announcer asked everyone to rise for the national anthem.

The crowd quieted and stood facing the large American flag which hung on the wall at one end of the court. The band began to play the "Star Spangled Banner."

Jack stood up straight and began to sing. He noticed that only a few people were singing, but this did not discourage Jack. He loved being an American, and he was proud to sing about his country.

The game began, and it was a thriller. Jack's school team won by two points, and everyone cheered enthusiastically when it was over.

On the way out of the gym, a tall man with snow white hair stopped Jack at the door. "Young man," he began, "I am Senator George White. I want to congratulate you on your loyalty to our country. I was impressed to hear you sing while so many around you were embarrassed to do so. I would like to shake your hand as a token of my appreciation."

Jack thanked the gentleman. It was special to be honored by the senator. It increased Jack's determination to be loyal to his country, even when others were not.

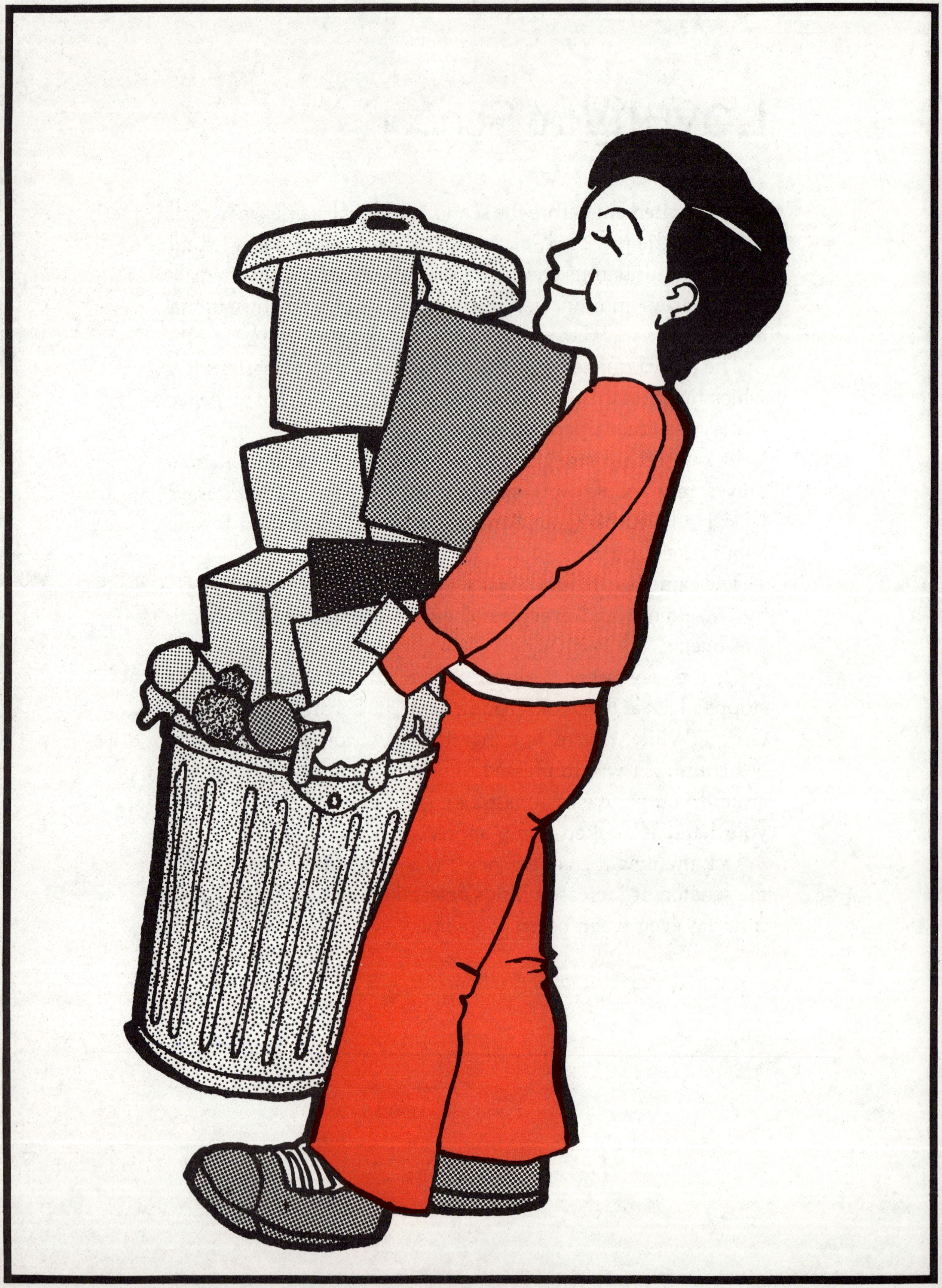

Responsible
full

Doing What I Know
I Ought to Do

Moreover it is required in stewards, that a man be found faithful.

1 Corinthians 4:2

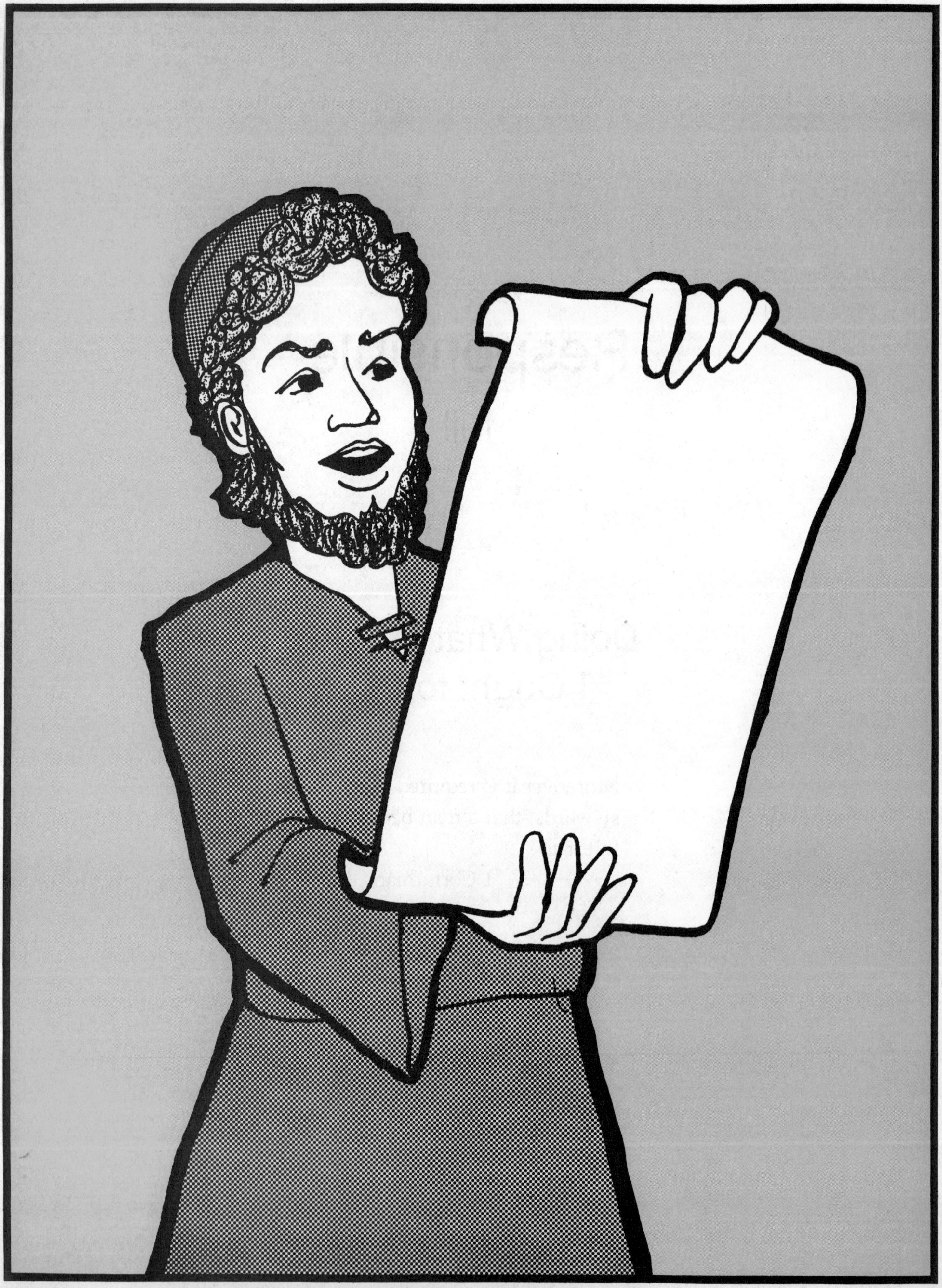

Responsibility in the Bible

The armies of Nebuchadnezzar had captured Israel and its king, Zedekiah. Large numbers of captives were marching on the road back to Babylon to become slaves. God's prophet, Jeremiah, stopped a man named Seraiah, who was Zedekiah's army quartermaster. He gave him a strange mission.

"Take this scroll," said Jeremiah quietly. "I have written upon it all the terrible things God is going to do to Babylon because of their wickedness."

Seraiah had great respect for Jeremiah and knew that God spoke through him. He accepted the scroll.

Jeremiah continued, "When you get to Babylon, read aloud to others what I have written. Tell those people that God will destroy Babylon so that not a living creature will escape alive. The great city will be abandoned forever. Do you understand my instructions?"

Seraiah nodded yes.

"One more thing," the prophet added. "When you have finished reading the scroll, tie a rock to it and throw it into the Euphrates River. Tell them that Babylon will sink and not rise, just like the rock and scroll that you throw into the water."

These words of the prophet would not be popular with his captors because they revealed the doom to come. But Seraiah believed that they were God's words, so he was responsible and did all that Jeremiah had instructed him to do.

This story is found in Jeremiah 51:59-64.

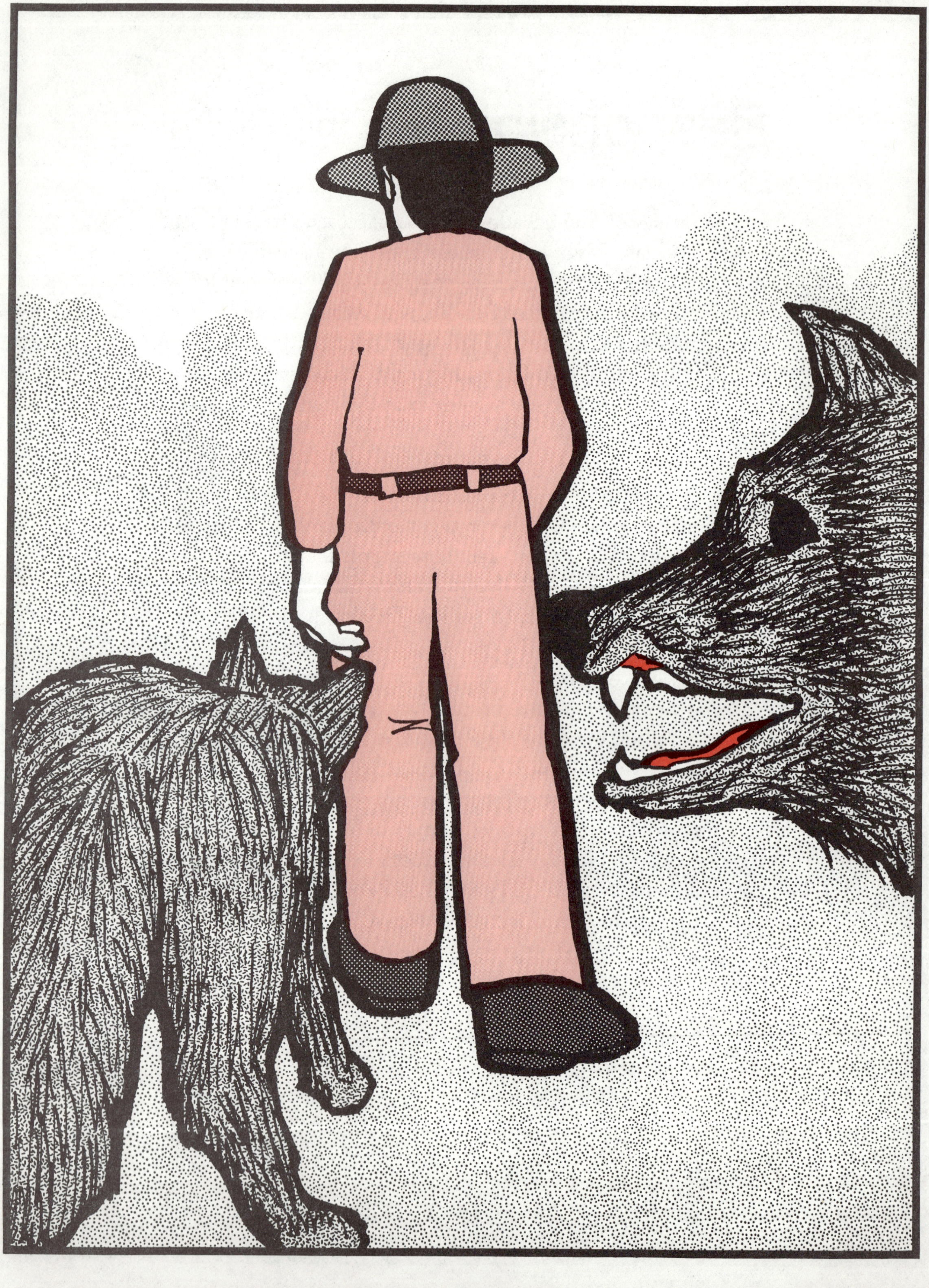

Responsibility
of a Hero of the Faith

The woods seemed strangely silent as the man walked alone. The path he traveled was seldom trod, because of the fierce dangers that lurked all around. This area was known to be infested with hungry wolves.

Missionary Andrew Murray had a church service to conduct. Since his horse had run away in fear of the wolves, Andrew would have to walk twelve or fifteen miles to the nearest farmhouse. He felt responsible to go, in spite of the dangers.

As Andrew walked he sensed he was not alone. Bushes began to rustle on either side of him. He began to pray.

After a few miles of stalking their prey, the wolves became bolder. They came out from hiding and began to follow him in the open. Andrew continued to pray and walk.

Some of the braver wolves trotted a few feet behind the missionary, snapping at his ankles. Andrew was afraid. God would have to show His mighty power now, or he would be killed and eaten.

For miles the wolves continued to growl and snap. Some even began to fight each other for the privilege of attacking the missionary first. Nevertheless, Murray continued praying all the way.

When he arrived at the farmhouse, the surprised farmer asked, "How did you do it? Where were the wolves?"

"They snapped at my ankles all the way," Andrew answered, "but they never touched me. I knew I had to get to that service, so I prayed to God to keep me, and He did."

Andrew Murray's sense of responsibility had placed him in a dangerous position, but God protected him as the missionary sought to do what he knew he ought to do.

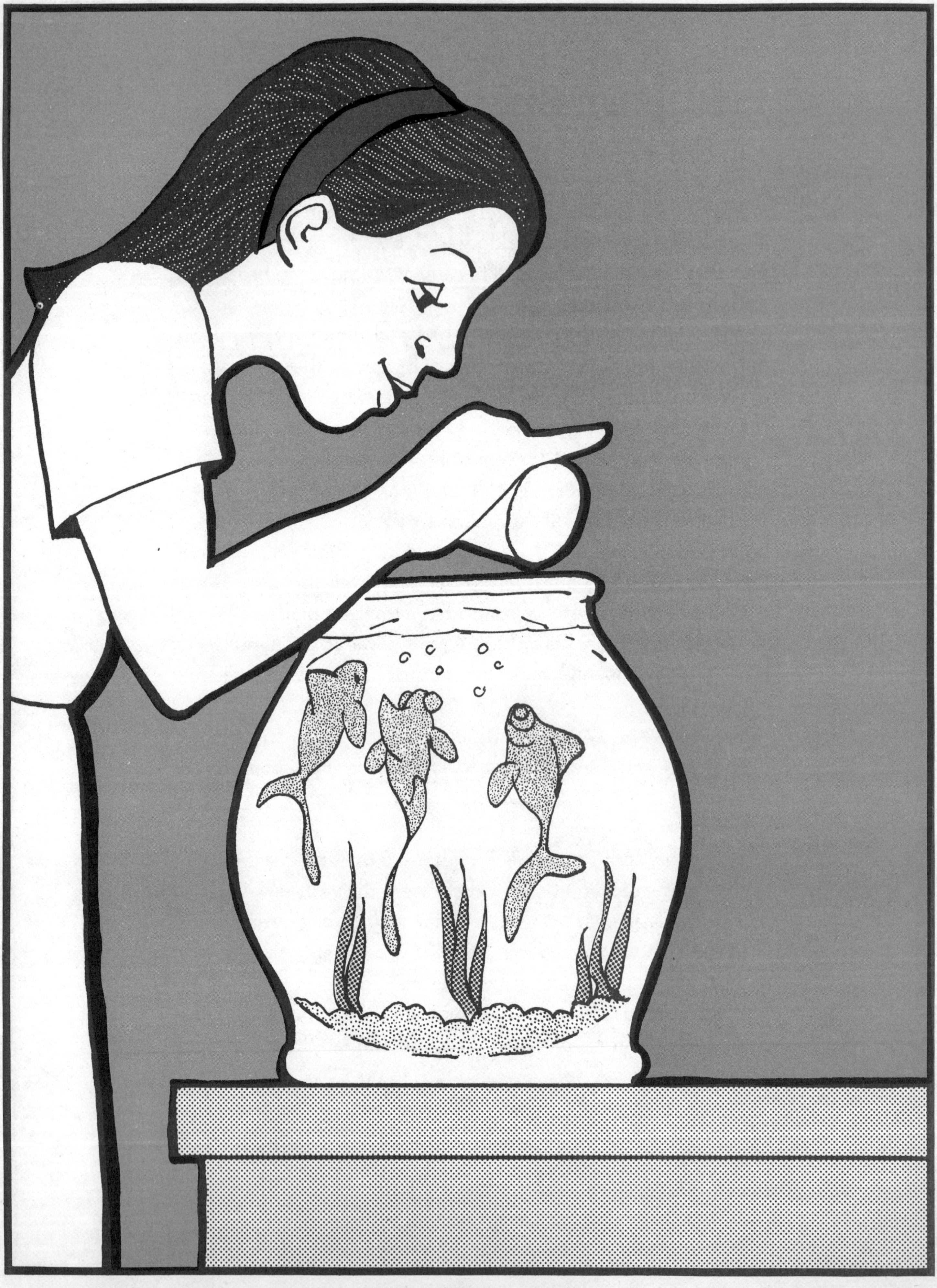

Responsibility at Home

Sara's eyes glowed with excitement as she watched her four goldfish dance in the bowl. Goldie, Spots, Big Eyes, and Fancy Fins were the names she chose for her fish.

Mother had a few words of caution. "Remember, fish are pets, just like dogs and cats. You must be responsible about feeding them regularly and keeping the fishbowl clean."

Sara agreed. She even made a chart that showed each day of the week and when she should feed the fish.

Weeks of enjoyment followed. Everyone in the family took time to watch the fish swim. However, as the weeks passed, Sara's interest in the fish began to wear off. Her chart showed that she did not always feed the fish on schedule or clean the fishbowl. The glass sides of the fishbowl began to get covered with a green plant material called algae.

One day a terrible thing happened. "Mother, Mother, Goldie is dead," cried Sara.

Mother paused and remembered her instructions as she hugged her daughter. "Sara, you have not been responsible about caring for your fish. When you don't do what you know you ought to do, there are consequences."

That day, Sara determined to be responsible with the rest of her fish.

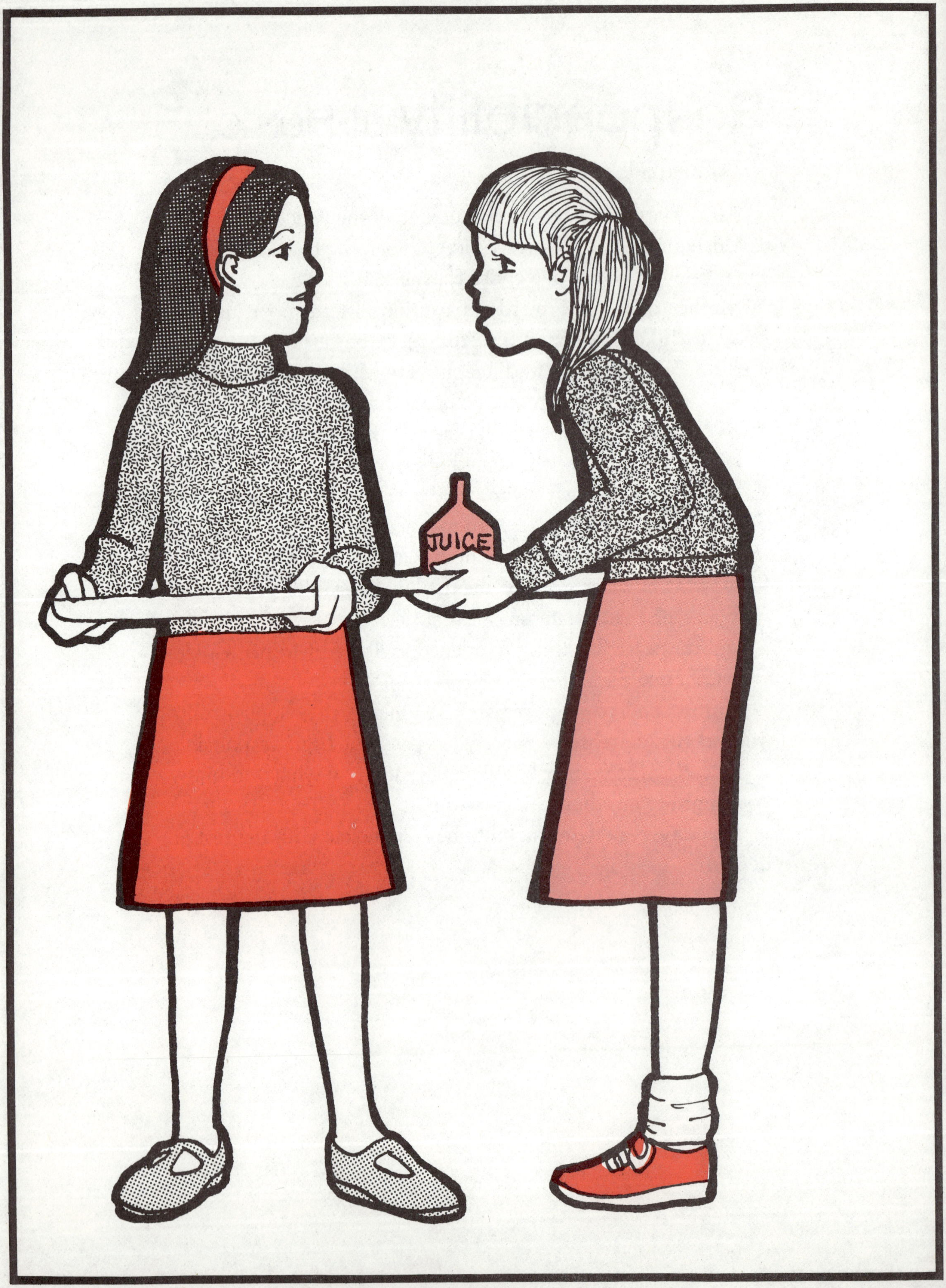
JUICE

Responsibility at School

Sara was very hungry. She had watched the clock all morning, while waiting for lunch. Her mother had packed a turkey sandwich, which she was looking forward to eating.

At last the bell rang. Everyone closed their books and got in line to buy their drinks.

Sara's friend Emily put a carton of orange juice on her tray. Turning to Sara she said, "Get the orange juice. It tastes so good."

"No, I can't," replied Sara. "Mother told me to buy milk today."

"Yes, you can," said Emily. "Your mother will never know which one you pick."

Sara had to make a quick decision. Should she be responsible and obey her mother, or should she please her friend? A scripture verse helped Sara decide what to do. She quoted it to herself. "The eyes of the Lord are in every place, beholding the evil and the good" (Proverbs 15:3).

Sara put a milk carton on her tray. "I would like very much to have orange juice with you, Emily, but I know it is not the responsible thing to do. God would know that I was not doing what I ought to do."

Emily looked disappointed. Yet she respected Sara's responsible attitude and was glad they were friends.

Character Development Challenges

This page is designed to give parents and teachers practical suggestions for teaching character traits to children.

Meekness

1. Psalms 37:1-11 gives a pattern for developing meekness. The student should memorize the passage, identifying the do's and don'ts contained in the verses.
2. Using the Book of Proverbs, the student should discover what the Bible says about anger.
3. Recall with the student a situation in which he was not meek. Discuss how a meek response would have given him better results.

Loyalty

1. To encourage loyalty to our country, have the student draw a replica of our flag on cardboard. Paint the flag. Glue popcorn where the stars and stripes should be. Review the meaning of each part of the flag:

   Fifty stars — one for each state
   Thirteen stripes — for the thirteen original states
   White — for freedom
   Red — for courage
   Blue — for loyalty

   List some ways to show loyalty to our country. (Answers may include voting, really meaning it as we sing the national anthem, not littering our land, and so on.)
2. At the end of the day, the child should review God's loyalty (faithfulness) to him (Psalms 92:2).
3. To encourage family loyalty, plan an activity that includes a younger sister or brother, especially on an occasion when friends are invited.

Responsibility

1. To encourage financial reponsibility, the child should be given an allowance. The money should be divided three ways: for the Lord, for savings, and for desires and needs. Using a notebook, he should keep a record of how the money was spent.
2. A weekly assignment should be given to the student, which would require him to find an answer to a Bible question. The answer could be given at family devotions or at the supper table.
3. The student should be given the responsibility of watering and nurturing a houseplant.